Just Like My Grandpa

Lada Kratky

Illustrated by José Ortíz

HAMPTON-BROWN BOOKS

MANY CULTURES, MANY LANGUAGES...MANY POSSIBILITIES!™

I love good food,
just like my grandpa.

I have a birthmark,
just like my grandpa.

I play music,
just like my grandpa.

I smile a smile,
just like my grandpa.

I wiggle my toes,
just like my grandpa.

I love my grandpa,
and my grandpa loves me.